The North American Indians

The
Apache

Titles in The North American Indians series include:

The Cherokee
The Comanche
The Iroquois
Native Americans of the Great Lakes
Native Americans of the Northeast
Native Americans of the Southwest
The Navajo
The Sioux

The North American Indians

The
Apache

Raymond H. Miller

KIDHAVEN PRESS

An imprint of Thomson Gale, a part of The Thomson Corporation

THOMSON

GALE™

Detroit • New York • San Francisco • San Diego • New Haven, Conn.
Waterville, Maine • London • Munich

LIBRARY OF CONGRESS CATALOGING-IN-PUBLICATION DATA

Miller, Raymond H., 1967–
  The Apache / by Raymond H. Miller.
    p. cm. — (North American Indians)
  Includes bibliographical references and index.
  ISBN 0-7377-2625-3 (hardcover : alk. paper)
  1. Apache Indians—History—Juvenile literature. 2. Apache Indians—Social life and customs—Juvenile literature. I. Title. II. Series.
  E99.A6M57 2005
  979.004'9725—dc22
                                    2004023570

Printed in the United States of America

Contents

Chapter One 6
Land of Apacheria

Chapter Two 14
Life Among the Apache

Chapter Three 22
Mythology, Spirits, and Ceremonies

Chapter Four 31
The Apache at War

Notes 42

Glossary 43

For Further Exploration 44

Index 45

Picture Credits 47

About the Author 48

Chapter One

Land of Apacheria

They are known as the Apache, but they refer to themselves as Ndee (in-DAY), which means "people." Historians believe the word *Apache* probably came from the Zuni Indian word *apachu,* meaning "enemy." The Apache earned this name because they were regarded as fierce warriors who often fought against the Zuni and other Native American groups centuries ago. The Apache descended from a group of people known as the **Athabaskans**. There is little in recorded history about this group of people, but it is thought that they were among the last group of Asians to come to North America thousands of years ago. Some historians believe they migrated across the Bering Strait along a narrow strip of land that once connected Asia and North America. The Athabaskans lived in Alaska and the Canadian Northwest for several thousand years.

The Athabaskans and other tribes living in that region of North America shared a common language, though each group probably had its own territory. In some instances conflicts erupted between the Athabaskans and the neighboring Inuit. However, it is believed that both groups lived somewhat peacefully side by side for many years.

The Athabaskans lived under very harsh conditions. Winter would have been especially difficult, with temperatures plummeting well below freezing. To stay warm

Before going to war, an Apache chief urges his warriors to fight bravely. The Apache were known for their fierceness in battle.

they bundled themselves in clothes made of animal fur and hide. In the summer they tracked and hunted caribou. They also set up fish camps to catch salmon.

South into Apacheria

Sometime after the 13th century a large group of Athabaskans left the frigid weather of winter and migrated several thousand miles south along the eastern side of the Rocky Mountains. According to Apache stories passed down over the years, most of the travelers ended up near what is now called Gobernador Canyon in present-day northwest New Mexico. Small groups of Athabaskan hunters continued to follow the same general route. They settled in what is now called the Four Corners

Four Corners

SOUTH DAKOTA

IDAHO   WYOMING

NEBRASKA

NEVADA

UTAH   COLORADO

KANSAS

CALIFORNIA

OKLAHOMA

Four Corners

ARIZONA   NEW MEXICO

Pacific
Ocean

TEXAS

MEXICO

region—where the borders of Arizona, Colorado, New Mexico, and Utah meet today.

The Athabaskan settlers eventually formed two main groups: the Apache and the Navajo. The Navajo became farmers in the Four Corners region. Meanwhile, groups of Apache wandered the land looking for places to live. Many settled in the Great Basin, Sonoran, and Chihuahuan desert regions. Others later scattered farther, settling in parts of what is now Kansas, Oklahoma, Texas, and northern Mexico. The land inhabited by the Apache was called Apacheria.

By the end of the 17th century there were seven Apache tribes. The Jicarilla, Kiowa-Apache, and Lipan tribes formed the Eastern Apache. The Navajo, Mescalero, Western Apache, and Chiricahua tribes made up the Western Apache. The names of some of the tribes were Native American words that describe the places where they lived. For example, historians Edwin R. Sweeney and Angie Debo write, "The word Chiricahua probably was derived from the Opata Indian word *chiguicagui*, meaning 'mountain of the wild turkeys.'" [1]

Scattered Bands

Unlike many other Native American tribes, the Apache never united as a single tribe. Even the seven individual groups that formed had little organization. There was no central tribal government or council. Instead, most Apache peoples lived in many loosely scattered groups within the seven branches. These groups were known as **bands**. Between two and six families, including grandparents, parents, unmarried children, and married daughters and their families, made up a band.

Each Apache band had its own **chief**, who provided strength and leadership to the people. He was often selected because he was a skilled hunter who could provide

Throughout the late 1800s, chief James A. Garfield led the Apache tribe known as the Jicarilla.

food for the people. The chief was also believed to possess spiritual powers and therefore could protect the band from harm. Sometimes several bands united under the different chiefs to hunt for food or to fight off invaders. But for the most part, each Apache band had its own territory for hunting, gathering, and farming.

On the Move

Life held many challenges for the Apache. Weather in the Southwest was harsh and often extreme. In the summer, hot, dry winds gusted up from the south. In the winter, cold winds blew down from the north. The Apache adapted to the changing seasons by wandering the rugged mountains and deserts as **nomads**. Everything they owned had to be carried from place to place. They usually set up camp near rivers or streams so they could be close to freshwater.

To shelter themselves from the severe heat and cold of the desert region, the Eastern Apache tribes built and lived in tepees. These cone-shaped structures were probably adapted from the tepees they observed the Plains Indians using. A tepee was made of wooden poles tied

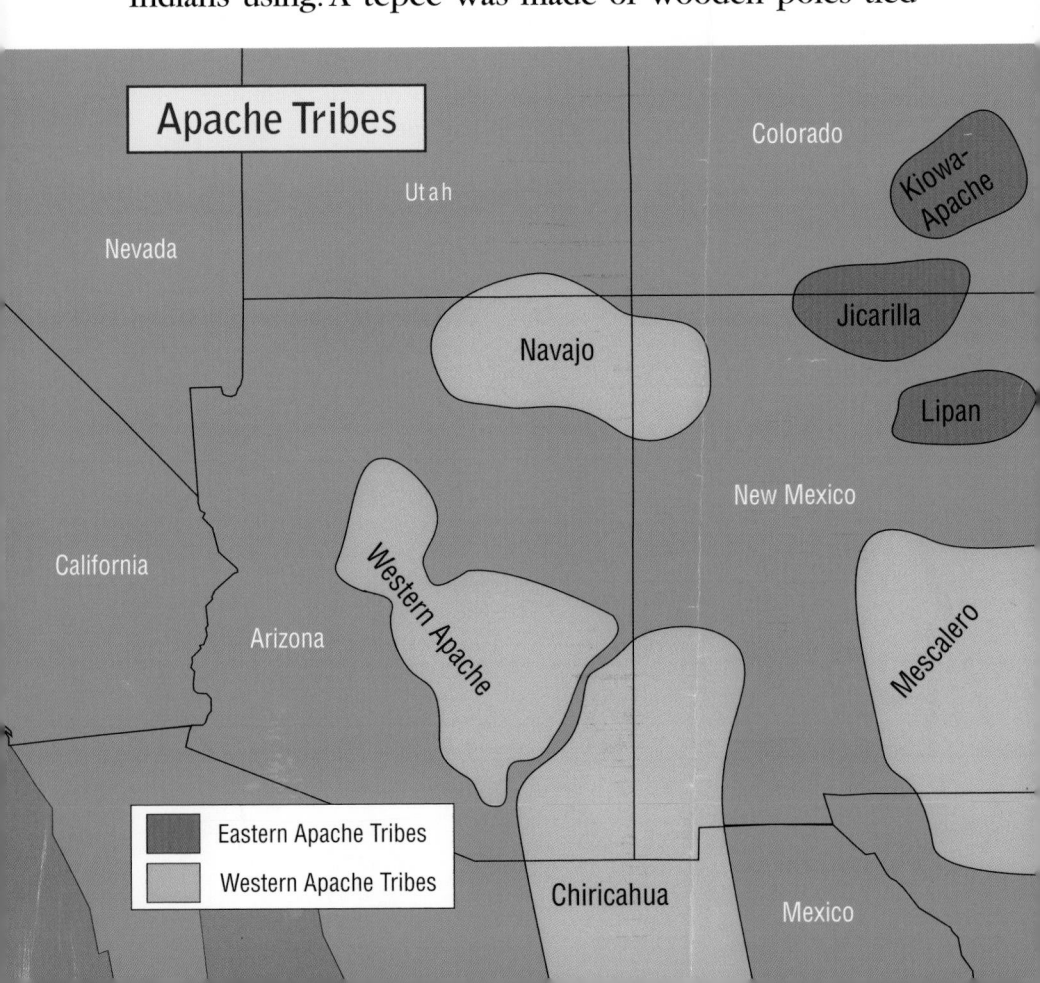

Apache Tribes

Colorado

Kiowa-Apache

Utah

Nevada

Jicarilla

Navajo

Lipan

New Mexico

California

Western Apache

Arizona

Mescalero

Eastern Apache Tribes

Western Apache Tribes

Chiricahua

Mexico

together at the top and wrapped with animal hides. The entire family lived in the tepee.

The Western Apache lived in structures called **wickiups**. To make a wickiup, the people set wooden poles firmly into the ground. The poles were bent over and tied together with strips of yucca leaf. In the summer, Apache women tied bunches of bear grass to the poles with yucca string to keep rain from entering. During the winter months, wickiups were covered with animal hides. Later, when the Apache began trading with European settlers and acquired canvas, wickiups were covered with this long-lasting material.

Wickiups were about 7 feet (2.1m) tall and ranged from 8 to 15 feet (2.4 to 4.6m) in diameter. Like tepees, wickiups provided enough space to house an entire family. There was no floor—just the ground that was packed

An Apache family poses at the entrance to their wickiup, a hut made from wooden poles covered with grass and animal hides.

hard and swept clean. For warmth, a fire was built in the middle of the wickiup. A small hole in the roof allowed the smoke to escape. Wickiups were easy to put up and take down, which was important to a group of people who sometimes packed up and moved as often as once every two weeks. Wickiups served another important purpose, too. Because Apache life was centered around the family, the wickiups were an ideal place for relatives to play, talk, and work together when the weather turned extreme in the land of Apacheria.

Chapter Two

Life Among the Apache

F amily was the most important aspect of Apache culture. Children were loved and cared for by parents, grandparents, and the other members of the band. Each family had a **headman**, usually the father, who made sure everyone followed the rules and did his or her part to help the group. The most important person in the household, though, was the mother.

Most Apache families were **matrilineal**, or connected through the mother's family. A daughter remained in her mother's home all of her life, just as her mother had done before her. Even after marriage, the daughter stayed home and her husband moved into her family's wickiup. The husband became a regular part of the family who hunted and worked alongside his wife's father and brothers. However, he did not speak to the mother and always bowed his head in her presence. These were traditional ways of showing great respect to a person. The wife's grandmother, who also lived with the mother's family, was especially highly regarded.

If a married daughter died, the widowed husband did not move out. He stayed and lived with her family, along with his children. His deceased wife's family provided him with a new bride, often another daughter or cousin. If the husband died, his wife was not bound to her husband's family in any way. His family could provide a cousin or brother for her to marry, but normally her own

Family was at the center of Apache culture. Here, an Apache chief poses with his wife and daughter.

family arranged another marriage. The new husband moved in to live with her in her family's wickiup.

Hunters and Gatherers

Every member of the family had a job to do, which was important because the Apache lived mainly as hunters and gatherers. From the Apache's earliest days in the desert plains, nomadic families and bands roamed the land trying to find enough food to survive. In the summer and fall, men hunted deer, rabbits, and other wild

Carrying her children on her back, an Apache woman joins her husband in the hunt for wild game.

Yndios Apaches.

game with bow and arrow in the more northern regions of Apacheria. When the men returned home from a successful hunt, the women cleaned the animals and preserved the meat through drying.

Women and children sometimes participated in a "surround hunt." They formed a huge circle in the woods or desert, then slowly walked toward the center, trapping rabbits and other small game animals inside. Women and children also gathered acorns, walnuts, cactus fruit, century plants, and a variety of other berries, nuts, roots, and seeds. They retrieved water and wood for cooking.

Although hunting and gathering provided most of their food, the Apache did not rely solely on these activities to survive. Author Sydele E. Golston notes, "The Apache also farmed small fields of corn, along with some beans and squash. The corn was planted in the spring; after summer forays for wild foods, the people returned in the fall to harvest the cornfields." [2]

After harvesting the crops, the Apache moved south to their winter camps, where temperatures were warmer. They survived on stored foods they had grown, gathered, or killed. In the spring they returned to the summer camps and began the harvesting cycle over again.

Transformed by the Horse

The Apache's nomadic ways remained largely unchanged for several hundred years. When Apache men set out on hunts, they rarely ventured very far from home. This was because they traveled on foot and had to carry anything they killed back to camp by hand. The introduction of the horse to the Southwest in the late 1600s changed the way the Apache hunted. It is believed the Apache acquired horses from Spanish traders who had traveled north into Apacheria from Mexico. With horses, the Apache could ride great distances and carry back much

Riding on horseback, an Apache hunter draws his bow as he takes aim at a buffalo.

more food. Some began ranging well into the Great Plains. There, they tracked herds of buffalo, which became a major source of food for them. Once the animals were in range, the Apache hunters shot them with bow and arrow, killing only what they needed to survive. After the hunters returned to camp, the meat was boiled, baked, roasted, or even eaten raw. Buffalo blood was cooked and thickened into soups, stews, and puddings.

The meat from buffalo and other animals was not simply eaten and the rest of the animal discarded. Bones were whittled into spoons and shaped into plates. Women and girls stretched and dried the hides of buffalo, antelope, deer, or elk to make a stiff, tough leather called **rawhide**. They rubbed and stretched the rawhide until it was soft and workable. Then they used their expert sewing skills to turn the leather into sturdy bags and blankets.

Clothing and Handicrafts

All of the clothes worn by members of a band were also made by hand. Men and boys wore long cloths made out of buckskin that were pulled between the legs and tied around the waist. This left two flaps hanging down to the upper thighs in the front and the back. Women and

This handmade Apache dress is made of buckskins sewn together and decorative beads.

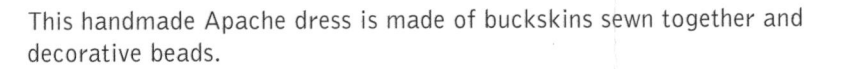

girls wore long skirts made out of buckskin. For shoes, Apache who lived in the desert wore tall leather moccasins to protect their feet and shins from cactus thorns and sharp rocks. Near or on the plains, Apaches wore low-cut moccasins.

Apache women also spent time making pottery and creating handicrafts such as drinking cups made out of hollowed-out gourds. But more than anything else they were known for their expert basket-weaving abilities. They wove beautiful baskets from plants, reeds, and herbs that grew wild in the desert and mountains or on the plains. They made four types of baskets: carrying baskets, storage jars, trays and bowls, and water jars covered with pinesap. The shapes of the baskets were similar, but

Apache women were known for their basket-weaving skills. Pictured is a woven bowl decorated with geometric designs.

the colors and designs of baskets varied from tribe to tribe. For example, the Western Apache's baskets were black and tan and had small coils. Baskets made by the Chiricahua and Mescalero were light green or brown because they were made with yucca leaves. Most baskets were decorated with geometric designs.

From crafting baskets and clothes to hunting and gathering food, the Apache demonstrated a keen ability to sustain themselves using what nature provided. They also showed the importance of working closely together within the band to survive. The Apache remained busy with their daily tasks, but they also took time to recognize and celebrate other things, such as ancient beliefs and rituals that had been passed down through the centuries.

Chapter Three

Mythology, Spirits, and Ceremonies

The Apache often remembered their origins through stories. One of the greatest tales of Apache mythology involves a woman named White Painted Woman. The Apache believed that in the beginning, the world was tormented by four monsters: Owl Man Giant, Buffalo Monster, Eagle Monster, and Antelope Monster. One day, the great spirit known as Life Giver approached White Painted Woman and told her that she would give birth to a son named Child Born of Water. After the child was born, White Painted Woman kept him safe by hiding him from the monsters.

In time, Child Born of Water told his mother that he was going to save the world by killing the monsters. Armed with his bow and arrows, he traveled deep into the woods and challenged Owl Man Giant to a shooting contest. Each was allowed to shoot four arrows at the opponent. Owl Man Giant was to shoot first, but before he could, Child Born of Water picked up a magical rock. He then used the rock to deflect all four arrows. Then it was Child Born of Water's turn. With his first three shots, he knocked away the top three layers of Owl Man

Giant's armor. His fourth shot pierced the monster's heart, killing it instantly. Child Born of Water later killed the other three monsters and returned to celebrate the feat with his mother. With the evil monsters destroyed, human beings were free to populate the Earth. For that reason, the Apache considered Child Born of Water to be their divine ancestor.

Good Spirits, Bad Spirits

While storytelling was a vital part of Apache custom, spirituality was also very important. They believed that every

The Apache believed that everything in nature contained a powerful spirit. Even the rising Sun had its own spirit.

object in nature—from the rising Sun to rocks, water, and air—contained an invisible but powerful spirit. They thought that by offering prayers to these objects, the spirits would bless them. For example, if the spirits were pleased by the Apache's prayers to the animals, they would provide food for the people in the form of buffalo, deer, or other wild game. The Apache also believed the spirits could weaken an enemy's strength or protect their people by preventing arrows from striking them during an attack. As a result, the Apache spent much time in prayer, hoping to be blessed by the many spirits.

The Apache also believed there were bad spirits or ghosts in nature, and the people feared being visited by these dark forces. Most of the evil spirits dwelled in certain animals, such as bears and coyotes. The Apache avoided these animals for this reason, but their greatest fear were of the spirit that lived in owls. The evil spirits of owls were thought to cause the worst kinds of diseases. If an owl was spotted near the camp, the Apache believed that sickness or even death would come to some member of their party.

Dance of the Gans

Above all of the spirits—good or bad—was the Great Spirit. Apache legend says that the Great Spirit sent the mountain spirits, called **Gans**, to help their people. The Gans taught them how to live a good and honorable life. They convinced the Apache to be good to one another, to care for the helpless, and to treat others with fairness. In doing these things, the Apache were protected by the Gans. The Apache also learned ceremonies and chants from the Gans. They began performing them to call for blessings from the Great Spirit. These included ceremonies in which the Apache prayed and chanted for the sick or injured to be healed. For many years, the legend

Wearing headdresses and body paint, three Apache men perform a dance in honor of the Gans spirits.

says, the Apache honored the Gans by following their great teachings. Eventually, however, the Apache people stopped performing the ceremonies, which angered the spirits. The Gans disappeared into the mountains, where they remained.

25

As the legend goes, the Apache attempted to regain the blessings of the Gans. They began performing one of the healing ceremonies they learned long ago. It was called the dance of the Gans. In the dance, masked dancers were painted in black, yellow, and white designs. They rhythmi-

An attendant massages an Apache girl during her Sunrise Ceremony, a ritual that welcomes her into womanhood.

cally circled one another around a roaring bonfire. They were led by a **medicine man**, who offered up songs to the spirits. As the dancers performed the ceremony, they touched the sick or wounded person with wands. They believed the illness was absorbed into the wands as they danced. The dance of the Gans is performed to this day at special ceremonies and tourist events.

Another important ceremony in Apache culture was the Sunrise Ceremony. It is believed White Painted Woman started this tradition long ago as a way to welcome Apache girls into womanhood. Many rituals made up this ancient ceremonial dance that lasted for four days and four nights. Dancers sprinkled sacred corn pollen and a woman attendant massaged the girl to make her posture straight and firm. The girl tossed a blanket in all four directions, beginning with the east. This symbolized the many blessings and wealth she would have wherever she went later in life. Like the dance of the Gans, the Sunrise Ceremony is still performed by the Apache today on special occasions.

Death and Burial

The Apache also had rituals concerning death. They believed that when a person died, his or her spirit or ghost hovered around the body before beginning the long journey to the underworld. According to Apache mythology, the person's ghost was led to the underworld by the ghosts of his or her relatives. Some Apache tribes believed the underworld consisted of two places. One part of the underworld was a peaceful green place inhabited by the ghosts of people who had been good all of their lives. The other part was a barren world reserved for the ghosts of people who had not been good in life.

People did not talk openly about the dead for fear of angering their ghosts. They spoke of a person's death

The Apache believed that, upon death, a person's ghost was led on a journey to the afterworld by the spirits of his or her relatives.

only with the brief phrase "He is gone."[3] Then they began a period of mourning in which they put on old clothing, cried loudly, and cut their hair. Relatives of the deceased held a special burial ceremony to speed the ghost's departure to the underworld. The relatives feared that if the ghost remained on Earth for very long, it would cause them harm.

Before the 16th century, the Apache simply placed the body in a cave or in a rocky crevice and left it. Family members destroyed all of his or her belongings. This was done to make sure the dead relative's ghost would not return to retrieve the items. After the Apache acquired

Always aware of the danger they faced, Apache warriors wore cloaks like this one painted with gods and spirits for protection from death.

horses, however, the dead person and all of his or her possessions were led away from the camp on horseback. Taking no chances, the Apache took down their tepees or wickiups and relocated to another campsite.

While the Apache feared death, it did not diminish their bravery in any way. They were fierce warriors who were unafraid to fight to the death against neighboring tribes and white people who dared to settle on their lands. In fact, warfare was a way of life for the Apache in a region that grew increasingly hostile in the 16th through 19th centuries.

Chapter Four

The Apache at War

From the Apache's earliest years in the Southwest, they were in frequent conflict with other Native Americans over territory and food. Therefore, the men had to be trained if they were expected to go into battle and survive. They developed warrior skills at an early age by being forced to spend many days at a time in the rugged desert or mountains. They were expected to live only on the food they could hunt and kill. During this time of intense training, the boys grew strong and built up incredible endurance. They were able to travel up to 70 miles (112.6 km) on foot in a single day. They were also trained to shoot a bow and arrow, and most became expert marksmen. If a boy could show he had mastered the necessary survival and fighting skills by age seventeen, he was allowed to join a **war party**. This was a group of men that went to battle against an enemy.

When the Apache had a reason to go to war, sometimes the bands united and sent as many as 200 warriors into battle. Before the arrival of the horse, the Apache conducted raids on foot. They often had to travel for days at a time across barren desert land before they reached their opponent. They preferred a fighting method that used elements of surprise. This included

Boys were trained at an early age to become warriors. Decorated with body paint, this boy is ready to go into battle.

hiding behind trees or large rocks, then attacking the enemy as they passed.

Fighting the Invasion

Starting in the mid-1500s, the Apache caught a glimpse of a future enemy. Spanish explorers from Mexico began entering Apache territory in their search for gold and other treasures. It was the Apache's first contact with white people and they were distrustful of their new neighbors. They moved their campsites from place to place to avoid contact.

But the Spanish kept coming and eventually set up **missions** in an attempt to convert the Apache and other native peoples to Christianity. For the next 60 years the two parties managed to live somewhat peacefully side by side. In that time Apache bands traded with the Spanish and acquired guns. They also acquired horses, which made them far more fearsome warriors. Now they could strike rival Native American groups from a distance and escape quickly.

In 1599 peace with the Spanish came to an end when the Apache helped defend the Pueblo Indians against Spanish attack. For most of the 1600s, the Apache raided Spanish settlements in hopes of driving the invaders away. No road or village was safe from attack. The Apache stole their enemy's livestock and horses. This in turn led to Spanish raids on the Apache. Spanish soldiers tied Apache men, women, and children together and marched them into Mexico, where they were sold as slaves.

In the late 1600s, the Jicarilla and Mescalero Apache— armed with guns—joined the Pueblo to drive the Spanish out of New Mexico. But the Apache soon found themselves facing another enemy: the Comanche. This fierce Native American tribe had moved southward into Apache territory from present-day Wyoming. Historian

Albert Marrin writes, "The Apache met their match in the Comanche. It was like bringing together fire and gunpowder. The moment they touched, warfare exploded between them." [4] The Apache fought bitterly against the Comanche, as well as Spanish soldiers, for most of the 18th century. Then, the Spanish and the Comanche joined forces to fight the Apache bands, who were still conducting raids against them. Many Apache bands were devastated by the fighting and eventually stopped the raids. Some bands settled in villages around the Spanish missions and the two sides lived together in peace. However, other Apache bands refused to give up and continued to attack anyone who entered their lands.

Geronimo and the Apache Wars

While bands of Apache struggled to ward off all invaders, Mexico was fighting a war of its own. The Mexican people fought for their independence from Spain, which had colonized Mexico in the early 16th century. Finally, in 1821 they gained that freedom, and the land the Apache called their own fell under Mexico rule. Mexican soldiers were sent to conquer the Native American groups living in the newly acquired territory. The soldiers were outnumbered and struggled in their quest to defeat the tribes. Seeking to gain control once and for all, the soldiers began paying Mexican hunters money in exchange for the scalps of Apache men, women, and children. This led to the massacre of many Apache people.

In 1846 the United States declared war on Mexico and won control of Apache territory in the present-day states of Arizona and New Mexico. The young nation was expanding westward and thousands of people flooded the lands the Apache had long considered their own. Once again the Apache fought back by launching furious raids against the white settlers. The U.S. government sent soldiers to set up military forts in Arizona and New Mexico to establish order. This led to a number of fierce clashes between U.S. soldiers and Apache warriors. These clashes became known as the Apache Wars.

During the Apache Wars, the great Chiricahua warrior Geronimo gained nationwide fame. His mother, wife, and

Armed with rifles, an Apache war party rides across the desert to meet the enemy in battle.

U.S. officers try to convince Geronimo (far left) to surrender in this 1886 photograph. The warrior became well known for his fierce fighting during the Apache Wars.

three daughters had all been killed by U.S. soldiers on the same day in 1852. Geronimo vowed to avenge their deaths by taking up arms against the U.S. Army and the white settlements. In the twenty-plus years that followed, he and his band of outnumbered warriors fought savagely against the trained soldiers. He avoided capture until 1874, when he was defeated and placed on a **reservation**. Geronimo escaped and hid for more than ten years in the mountains of Mexico. He frequently raided the white people living across the border.

Finally on August 25, 1886, Geronimo surrendered to the U.S. Army in Arizona. He and his fellow warriors were sent to a reservation in Florida before being taken to Fort

Sill, Oklahoma, where they were held as prisoners of war. Curious people all over the United States wanted to see the famous warrior. Government officials frequently allowed him to appear in Western shows across the country. He even rode in the inaugural parade of President Theodore Roosevelt in 1905.

Geronimo led a band of Apache warriors that fought the U.S. Army for more than twenty years.

This photograph taken in 1886 shows Geronimo (first row, third from right) with fellow Apache prisoners outside a train car destined for a Florida reservation.

Most other Apache were not so fortunate. As more and more white settlers moved into the Southwest, the U.S. government rounded up the remaining Apache people and isolated them on reservations. For the most part, conditions on the reservations were miserable. The Apache suffered from malnutrition and poverty. Tuberculosis, a highly contagious disease that affects the lungs, was also a problem. The disease was so bad among the Jicarilla that 90 percent of the schoolchildren contracted it. By 1920 the Jicarilla population was cut nearly in half.

The Apache Today

Conditions began to improve for the Apache in 1924 when they and other Native Americans were granted U.S. citizenship. In the decades that followed, the Apache also gained civil rights. Though the U.S. government did

Today, most Apache, like this young man dancing in a ceremony, are very proud of their cultural heritage.

not return their land, in 1970 the Apache were awarded nearly $10 million in exchange for their losses. The Apache used this money to build new schools, hospitals, and other public facilities.

Today there are three main Apache tribes: the Chiricahua, the Eastern Apache, and the Western Apache. The

An Apache dresses in traditional clothing for an Inauguration Ceremony on the White Mountain, Arizona, reservation, one of three in Arizona belonging to the Western Apache.

Chiricahua continued to live in Oklahoma after Geronimo and others were relocated there. The Eastern Apache, which is made up of descendants of the Jicarilla and Mescalero bands, reside in New Mexico. And the Western Apache live on three separate reservations in Arizona. Most Apache have embraced all aspects of American culture. They speak English, live in modern homes, and wear the latest fashions. They work in many different fields, including business, cattle ranching, politics, and teaching. Even so, today's generation of Apache people are determined to never forget their ancestors. Most choose to balance their new way of life with Apache beliefs, traditions, and spirit that have long defined this Native American people.

Notes

Chapter One: Land of Apacheria
1. Edwin R. Sweeney and Angie Debo, *Great Apache Chiefs: Cochise and Geronimo.* New York: MJF Books, 1991, p. 3.

Chapter Two: Life Among the Apache
2. Sydele E. Golston, *Changing Women of the Apache.* New York: Grolier, 1996, p. 104.

Chapter Three: Mythology, Spirits, and Ceremonies
3. Raymond Bial, *The Apache.* New York: Benchmark, 2001, p. 44.

Chapter Four: The Apache at War
4. Albert Marrin, *Plains Warrior: Chief Quanah Parker and the Comanches.* New York: Atheneum, 1996, p. 37.

Glossary

Athabaskans: A group of Asian people that migrated to North America many thousands of years ago; ancestors of the Apache.

bands: Groups of two to six families living within an Apache tribe.

chief: A Native American leader.

Gans: Spirits the Apache people believe were sent to give them instruction; also known as mountain spirits.

headman: The male leader of a Native American family.

matrilineal: Family descent based on the maternal line.

medicine man: A religious healer.

missions: Churches or other religious establishments used to convert people to Christianity.

nomads: People who have no permanent home and wander from place to place.

rawhide: Tough leather made from animal hide.

reservation: Land set aside to keep Native Americans together.

war party: A group of Native Americans that went to war.

wickiups: Huts made from natural materials such as wooden poles, grass, and yucca leaves.

For Further Exploration

Books

Craig A. Doherty and Katherine M. Doherty, *The Apaches and Navajos.* New York: Franklin Watts, 1989. An excellent beginner's guide to these two famous Native American peoples.

Editors of Time-Life Books, *Native Americans.* Alexandria, VA: Time-Life Books, 1995. Explores in detail where Native American Indians came from, what they wore, how they celebrated, and more. Filled with full-color photos, maps, and illustrations.

Barbara McCall, *Native American People: The Apaches.* Vero Beach, FL: Rourke, 1990. Examines all aspects of Apache life, from their early days of hunting and gathering to life on the reservation. Includes important dates in Apache history.

Patricia McKissack, *A New True Book: The Apache.* Chicago: Childrens, 1984. Examines the fascinating story of the Apache in an easy-to-read style.

Web Site

Smithsonian: American Indian History and Culture (www.si.edu/history_and_culture/american_indian). An excellent source for information about Native American Indians. Includes biographies, photos, interactive maps, and much more.

Index

Apacheria, 9
Apache Wars, 34–36
Athabascans, 6–9

bands, 9–10, 31
baskets, 20–21
beliefs
  about death, 27–30
  about spirits, 22, 23–27
buffalo, 18
burials, 29–30

ceremonies, 24–27, 28–29
chiefs, 9–10
Child Born of Water,
  22–23
Chiricahua (tribe)
  area of, 9
  baskets of, 21
  currently, 40–41
Christianity, 33
clothes, 7–8, 19–20
Comanche (tribe), 33–34

death, 27–30
Debo, Angie, 9
disease, 38

Eastern Apache, 9, 40–41

family, 13–16
farming, 17
food, 8, 17
Four Corners region, 8–9

Gans (mountain spirits),
  24–27
Geronimo, 35–37
Gobernador Canyon, New
  Mexico, 8
Golston, Sydele E., 17
government, 9–10
Great Spirit, 24

headmen, 14
homes, 11–13, 30
horses, 17–18, 30
hunting, 8, 16–18

Inuit, 6–7

Jicarilla (tribe)
  area of, 9
  currently, 41
  tuberculosis and, 38
  warfare and, 33

Kiowa-Apache (tribe), 9

legends, 22–23, 24–27
Life Giver, 22
Lipan (tribe), 9

Marrin, Albert, 34
medicine men, 27
men, 16–18, 19
Mescalero (tribe)
  area of, 9
  baskets of, 21
  currently, 41
  warfare and, 33
Mexicans, 34
missions, 33
mythology, 22–23, 24–27

names, 6, 9
Navajo (tribe), 9
Ndee, 6
nomadic lifestyle, 11

origin myth, 22–23
Owl Man Giant, 22–23
owls, 24

Pueblo (tribe), 33

rawhide, 18
religion
  Christianity, 33
  death and, 27–30
  spirits and, 22, 23–27
reservations, 36, 38
rituals, 24–27, 28–29

Spaniards, 17, 33

spirits, 22, 23–27
Sunrise Ceremony, 27
surround hunts, 17
Sweeney, Edwin R., 9

tepees, 11–12, 30
tribes, 9, 40–41
  see also specific tribes
tuberculosis, 38

underworld, 27, 28–30
United States
  Apache as citizens of,
    39–41
  reservations, 36, 38
  warfare against, 34–36

warfare, 30–31, 33–36
Western Apache
  area of, 9
  baskets of, 21
  currently, 40–41
White Painted Woman, 22,
  27
wickiups, 12–13, 30
women
  clothes of, 19–20
  hunting and, 17
  importance of, in family,
    14–16
  items made by, 18, 20–21
  Sunrise Ceremony and,
    27

Zuni, 6

Picture Credits

Cover Image: © Corbis
AP/Wide World Photos, 26, 39
© Archivo Iconografico, S.A./CORBIS, 16
© Tom Bean/CORBIS, 40
© Bettmann/CORBIS, 10, 15, 36, 37
© Bowers Museum of Cultural Art/CORBIS, 20
© Christie's Images/CORBIS, 28
© Geoffrey Clements/CORBIS, 18
© CORBIS, 12, 32, 38
Corel Corporation, 23
© Werner Forman/Art Resource, NY, 29
© Charles & Josette Lenars/CORBIS, 25
© Mary Evans Picture Library, 7, 35
Museum of the American Indian, 19

About the Author

Raymond H. Miller is the author of more than 50 nonfiction books for children. He has written on a range of topics from poisonous animals to presidential trivia. He enjoys spending time outdoors with his wife and two daughters, including visiting the ancient Seminole Indian grounds near his home in Florida.